YOU AND ME

FRIENDSHIP
THROUGH THICK AND THIN

JAMES RAY ASHURST, Ph.D.

WESTBOW
PRESS®
A DIVISION OF THOMAS NELSON
& ZONDERVAN

WestBow Press books may be ordered through booksellers or by contacting:

WestBow Press
A Division of Thomas Nelson & Zondervan
1663 Liberty Drive
Bloomington, IN 47403
www.westbowpress.com
1 (866) 928-1240

Scripture taken from the King James Version of the Bible.

ISBN: 978-1-6642-0041-8 (sc)
ISBN: 978-1-6642-0040-1 (hc)
ISBN: 978-1-6642-0042-5 (e)

Library of Congress Control Number: 2020913829

Print information available on the last page.

WestBow Press rev. date: 08/05/2020

ACKNOWLEDGMENTS

I want to thank the following three individuals
for their tremendous assistance in contributing
to the information in this book:

Ms. Amy Grice

Ms. Lu Ann Head

Ms. Zoe Sanchez

You made this book come to life.

Thank you.

Starting with book one, I have indeed been fortunate to have competent proofreaders. For a person to read carefully every line in a book requires patience, care, perseverance, and commitment. It is certainly not a glorious job, but it is of utmost importance. In this book, I give praise to the following individuals for the professional "job" that they accomplished:

Ms. Carolyn Baker

Ms. Joy Breedlove

Ms. Gina Donahue

Ms. Sandy Bell

The phenomenal cover of this book was created by a genius of photography, *Chris*

Hefferen. If you were drawn to the cover, the credit entirely belongs to him.

During my lifetime, I have had wonderful

friends who have had a great positive impact

on my life. This book is dedicated to those

individuals.

CONTENTS

Acknowledgments v

Chapter 1   Friendship 1

Chapter 2   True Friendship 7

Chapter 3   The Powerful Element 11

Chapter 4   An Enduring Friendship 15

Chapter 5   The Sneaky Visitor... 21

Chapter 6   The Chasing Waiter 25

Chapter 7   Jacob 29

Chapter 8   The Neighbor Comrade...................................... 33

Chapter 9   Self-Esteem 37

Chapter 10   Effective Communication................................... 47

Chapter 11   Loneliness.. 53

Chapter 12   Life Happens 61

Chapter 13   Testimonies of Friendship 65

Chapter 14   Sarah and Her Loneliness 71

Chapter 15   God-Sent.. 77

Chapter 16   Toxic Relationships.. 81

Chapter 17   Becoming 89

Chapter 18   Mindfulness 95

Chapter 19   God In A Relationship... 99

Conclusion 103

Bibliography...105

CHAPTER 1

Friendship

When I arrived at the idea for another book, my first consideration was to see how much had already been written on the topic. Research is vital to me if I am planning on delving into the depths of the subject.

The idea surrounding the dynamics of a true, valid friendship has possessed my thinking process for quite some time. I can't seem to erase the continual, on-going mental possession of what valuable friendship involves. Even though I'd like to place the ideas on my mental back-burner to permit myself a short term breather, my mentality will not give my thinking process the permission to do so.

Hunting for research regarding the dynamics involving the value system of friendship has had its challenges. My happy thumb pressed the Amazon button with a positive outlook that surely I'd find a treasure of adult books on friendship. Thank goodness one can locate several such gems of literary wisdom. However, there are still not that many genuine, authentic books on friendship.

The list has not really touched the hem of the garment as far as the written work is concerned.

We throw the word "friendship" around as if every person we meet is a dear pal. Everybody in the neighborhood is our bosom pal, even though he or she just recently moved into our community.

"Let's find out the family's birthdays so we won't be humiliated."
"Mercy me! What in the world will we get them
for Christmas? It's just six days from today."
"We must throw them a party. Their anniversary is December 28."

You may be laughing or shaking your head at such comments because you have "friends" who are guilty of such.

And then the opposite scenario might well happen. Being normal human beings, at times we can find ourselves being desperate and partly obsessed with the idea of needing to claim to everyone that we have a multiplicity of intimate friendships. We seek to impress others, rather than be honest and real about our relationships with others.

There are many expressions that encompass one of the most treasured words in our complex language: **Friendship**. Trustworthy, Honesty, Authentic, Affection, Companion, Bond, Support, and Love.

Friendships are vital to have in an individual's life. They provide comfort, joy, stability, and even sanity. Such solid relationships will last a lifetime because a heritage has been created once the friendship is ignited.

We'll be friends until we're old and senile.
Then we'll be new friends.

---anonymous

Individuals in a strong relationship find immense pleasure in knowing each other—visiting with one another, talking over the phone, laughing together, being silly with each other, and sharing things that will remain confidential due to the mutual respect and admiration involved in the friendship. It's as if they can read each other's mind at times. It's a tenacious friendship that can hardly be destroyed. Such a strong bond adds validity, warmth, and love that will see one another through thick or thin—during troubles and successes. This kind of an authentic relationship lasts for decades, sometimes even until death.

In any relationship, each person receives different things out of it—needs, desires, and commitments. It is an awesome feeling knowing one has a unique connection that flows from one warm human body to another. One may not exactly be able to pinpoint the feeling that one has in a relationship, but one can just sense the enrichment that accompanies the phenomenal connection. There is a definite emotional investment as the relationship becomes deeper by means of learning about one another, growing emotionally together, and inspiring each other to become even greater and more successful than one already is.

A friend can tell you things you don't want to tell yourself.

----Frances Ward Weller

Even when we hit a rough spot in our life journey, the close friend has been by our side. The individual has been our support system, and we know such a truth due to all the hours one has spent with us while we have crawled through the heartaches and brokenness. Regularly, our friend has been in touch, encouraging us to "hang in there" through the mental and emotional storm of despair. The special friend reaches out to us in compassion at those critical times when we feel deserted and extremely alone. Leave it to those in our close relationships to find ways to meet our needs when we are combating the life trials that we all go through from time-to-time. Our friends, at such times, contribute to our well-being by means of positive thoughts, encouragements, and personal visits of support.

One of the many things I like about the close friends I have is the freedom I give them to challenge my thought processing. They are not hesitant or reluctant to pose questions to my ideas, comments, and present and future goals. When friends are free to do so, their thoughts provide an understanding of ourselves—their comments can stop us dead in our tracks, and our minds are opened in a way we hadn't possibly considered. What a remarkable balance is afforded to us: the balance between what we think and what our close friends offer

CHAPTER 2

True Friendship

When you can take off your shoes and prop your feet on a stool in a friend's home without your friend having a hissy fit, you are probably in the company of a special person in your life. When you aren't in the mood to be having a conversation and your friend is not offended or upset, you are more than likely in the presence of a special individual. A close friend can be as quiet as in the dead of night, or as loud as clowns in a circus. A friend feels comfortable without any attachments of tension or chaos. The relaxation is a dominant feeling between friends who are in a close relationship.

One of the most valuable relationships that we can have during our lifetime is our friendship with another individual. It is priceless, never to be confused with an acquaintance. This book describes what a genuine friend is and what attributes make up such a relationship. You will be able to distinguish the difference between a friend versus an acquaintance.

Valid friendships are as important as drinking water for a thirsty individual. Friendships offer us unconditional acceptance, emotional support, and mental uplifting challenges. All of these are important and what we need from day-to-day to keep us alert, sharp, and empathetic towards others. We all experience disheartening situations at times in our lives from our chaotic and stressful society. Thus, having genuine friends can enable us to see the sunshine behind the murky clouds of despair, hopelessness, and depression. Because each of us has such days, our relationship with the friends we have can deliver us to a mentally and emotionally safe spot of comfort and of peace. Thank goodness for his or her presence in our arena. Our arena can become quite desolate and lonely if we have isolated ourselves away from the loving-kindness and genuine love of a friend. Only having acquaintances in our arena just doesn't cut it.

Because friendships are based on our human needs, there will be misunderstandings at times. However, if the friendship is real and valid, we will figure out what happened, apologize if we were in the wrong, and re-establish the relationship—and keep moving forward, hand-in-hand with our friend. The key element is to figure out what caused the misunderstanding and attempt to "fix it" as soon as possible. All friendships can be repaired if the individuals want to restore them.

The relationship that may not have a chance is the one in which one of the friends attempts to control the other. It's called the "suffocation factor" by which one tries to be dominant over the other. Friendships cannot flourish when manipulation is a part of the relationship. Wanting to do such is selfish and destructive. Mentally and emotionally healthy individuals are neither controllers nor victims in the relationship.

In wonderful functioning friendships, there is no responsibility on anyone's part to try changing the other. That is a big NO-NO. It is not to be a part of the relationship. However, if one asks for some guidance from the other, be very, very careful. You and I are skating on thin ice. Making suggestions may be somewhat tolerable, but must be carefully done—very carefully. Attempting to alter the core personality of a friend raises a fat red flag. Much too risky.

The real test of a genuine friendship is if you can make an emergency call freely to your friend at 1:00AM or even later. (Did I just hear a gasp?) It is a true evaluation of the caliber of an honest-to-goodness friendship. I wouldn't recommend such being done on a regular basis. However, there are times when our world seems to be falling apart during the night, and our need to talk or to make a visit becomes overwhelming. If your friend is Johnny-on-the-spot at that time with you, then be certain to nurture that relationship because it is as precious as a valuable gem.

**True friendship comes when the silence
between two people is comfortable.**

---David Tyson

CHAPTER 3

The Powerful Element

A powerful element in any friendship is the devotion that each gives to the other. It is knowing that one's special friend will have "one's back" through thick and thin. Such a person is a 24/7 presence in one's life and will continue to be so. Because of the strong devotion, the importance of the relationship is on the highest level. Priority #1 is given to the relationship, and each person knows it. What a great feeling to know actually that one has top priority in someone else's arena! When times get rough, we know for a fact that we have special persons who will help us through them. When times are going well, we have the same individuals who are wishing us the very best and are our cheerleaders. And it is a two-way street. We are to treat them the same.

These lifelong relationships add stability and happiness in our lives. With the stressors we encounter in maintaining everyday activities, we need and want friendships that can help us remain stable without our going off the deep end. We need positive reinforcements from our friends because life can be very hectic and chaotic at times. All of us need help during these long moments.

When was the last time you gave your friend(s) a heartfelt compliment? If you are a man, it was probably during the dinosaur age. We men have trouble in this life category. Because we live in such a busy technological world, we sometimes forget or are embarrassed to do a very crucial thing in our relationships: giving each other a pat-on-the-back. Handing out verbal warm fuzzies does both parties good. The one receiving the compliment is enhanced, and the one giving it can feel he or she has shed light into someone's life. Everyone can benefit emotionally by being praised from time to time.

The deepest principle in human nature is the craving to be appreciated.

---William James

Genuineness

If a friendship is to flourish, it must be given a top priority status. It cannot be placed on the back burner and given proper attention when convenient. The friendship is based on a mutual love for one another. It is a feel-good relationship. The friends encourage each other to reach life goals and to become quality-oriented individuals. The idea of friendship is to encourage the individual to remain unique, not to conform to what others want. If we encourage the person's uniqueness, we are promoting his or her self-esteem, self-worth, and self-image. When life's circumstances are pounding the one, then the other is to be an encouraging agent—hanging out with that person if possible—side-by-side.

When a relationship becomes a genuine friendship, there occurs a remarkable acceptance of each other. There is no critical confrontation of trying to change bits and pieces of the friend's personality. Accepting the individual, as is, is the dynamic that attracted your establishing the relationship in the first place. We are to allow each person to be who he or she is. If any changes need to be made, I suggest looking in the mirror. One's integrity is at stake. If the friend asks about one's personality traits, then the door is open, but tread very, very softly and carefully! Remember, you and I are messing with their personhood—their integrity. Bestowing affirmation regarding their sense of integrity enhances the friendship to greater heights.

No matter how solid our self-esteem is, if we are honest, all of us desire and appreciate praise. It reaffirms our self-esteem, self-worth, and self-image. It is not a matter of conceit but rather a good solid feeling to know that someone thinks highly of us. When we are abundant in giving compliments to another individual, not only do we feel good, even proud at times in doing so, but the other person also receives a wonderful feeling—a pat-on-the-back. It doesn't cost us one cent to praise another individual, but we do receive an abundant harvest of multiple positive emotions. Try and see for yourself.

It's the unexpected kindness (praise) from the unexpected person at the unexpected moment that makes someone feel special.

--anonymous

There is a wonderful magic that goes into formulating a relationship called friendship. The magic formula can be listed as follows:

    *Spend quantity time with one another.
    *Be honest with your feelings and thoughts.
    *Go places together.
    *Stay in continual contact.
    *Have fun with one another.
    *Compliment each other—lift up one another.
    *Respect the integrity of the other.
    *Apologize when necessary.
    *Share memories.
    *Protect one another emotionally.

CHAPTER 4

An Enduring Friendship

The friendship was bound to happen. It was inevitable. And that it did. Mark and Jane grew up together—they were neighbors. They played together, acted goofy, laughed uncontrollably at times. They celebrated one another's birthdays in fine style. When you saw one, you saw the other. Their bond was tenaciously strong. Spending time together was always a blast. No one dared to hurt or to say anything derogatory about the other unless the person wanted a fist fight to erupt.

Mark and Jane had an authentic friendship which included defending one another and standing up for each other, even in front of a teacher. Each had the magic of calming down the other when life didn't go the way he or she expected, and each would call upon the other's strength of character to muddle through the ordeal. They were genuine companions.

The time for college came much too soon in their opinion. How did elementary, middle, and high school go so fast? Each had decided on a different college, not far from each other. Their last summer before heading to college was spent together, almost 24/7. They did everything with one another, maintaining their strong bond. They traded ideas of what to do together, so multiple adventures occurred.

They each had to leave on the same day for college. It was a gloomy, rainy day which certainly didn't help the situation. While the parents and siblings were saying their good-byes, Jane and Mark remained side-by-side. Tears flooded over their faces. Their hearts were breaking, and the agony was horrible.

For each, the drive to college seemed endless. However, they promised to remain in contact and that they did. Letters, phone calls, and texts kept them up-to-date on each other's life events.

Their final year of college approached, and the relationship was as strong as ever since they had been together during breaks and summers.

Christmas was a humdinger. So much fun. They decided to attend the same college for their masters' degrees. All was set. When the holidays were over, they both returned to their colleges for their final semester, looking forward to being together again during the summer.

Mark, you are looking peaked. Are you okay?"
"Yeah, just tired. I'll be fine."

Jane became a little concerned about Mark when she hadn't heard from him in several weeks since her return to campus. But she chalked it up to his busy academic schedule during his last semester as a senior.

Several more weeks passed and still no word from her best friend. Late one evening, Jane had an unsettling feeling about Mark. She made a call to Mark's parents in order to calm down her worries.

Finally their phone was answered.

"Ms. Fitzgerald, this is Jane. I've not heard from Mark in weeks. I can't even reach him by phone. Is he doing okay?"

(there was a long pause)

"Jane, he is very sick. He's here at home. He didn't want to worry you, so he asked us not to call you or even tell your parents."

"What's wrong? Is he hurting? What's going on?"

"Mark has terminal cancer!" (the mother begins sobbing softly) *"If you can, you need to come as soon as possible. Mark's dying."*

The shock was more than Jane could handle. Her whole body began shaking violently, tears gushed from her eyes. She tried screaming but no words could come out. She saw her whole world crumble.

Within 30 minutes, she was heading home. She went directly to Mark's house where the atmosphere was dreary and morose... almost frightening.

Jane could not believe what she saw when looking at her dear pal. His once handsome body was grossly emaciated. His body was wasting away. His gaunt look made him look famished. All she saw was skin-and-bones.

(gently speaking) *"Hey, cowboy."*

(opening his eyes) *"Well, hey girl."*

Jane placed her trembling hand on his lanky hand.
No one spoke for a while.

"Jane, try not to weep too much. You know what a mess your face can become."

"Oh, hush up. I'll weep as much as I want."

"Jane, you know I've been in love with you since forever."

"Yes, I know. And I've loved you longer than forever."

"Jane, cherish our memories together. Remember all the laughs and goofy things we did. There are no regrets. I've loved every minute of our times together."

"Mark, you've always been my hero. You've allowed me to be your shadow. You have been the wind beneath my wings all these wonderful years. You are the one who has been my cheerleader, who has encouraged me to try different things. I love you, Mark Fitzgerald."

"And I love you. I'm tired and need some sleep. I'll see you tomorrow. I promise."

Jane leaned over and kissed her best friend on the forehead.

She was unable to sleep because of the continuous tears flooding her eyes all night.

The next morning seemed to take forever to arrive.

As soon as she entered his house, she knew.
He was unable to keep his promise.
She would never see her hero again on earth.
He would not be at her graduation.
And she would never have such a genuine,
authentic pal like him again.

Not all friendships last for multiple decades. Some are brief but still powerful. One cannot measure friendships by how long they last, but rather by the moments of kindness and love that are bestowed on each other, regardless of the time given to each one by God.

You can win more friends with your ears than your mouth.

----Anonymous

CHAPTER 5

The Sneaky Visitor

The year was 1963. Being president of my sophomore class in college kept me hopping in addition to numerous other extracurricular activities. Also, my taking 19-hour-course credits was definitely an idea on the dumb side. The beginning of my back pain was simply annoying at first, until…

The night it came to a head still lingers. The pain jarred me into consciousness from what started as a semi-peaceful slumber. Waking my parents prompted a call the next morning to our physician. After all was said and done (x-rays), the diagnosis was spontaneous pneumothorax, which is a fancy term for collapsed lung. Off to the hospital my mom and I traveled. The stay in the hospital was three long days, hooked up to a machine that would slowly and gradually inflate my lung once again.

It was during my time in the hospital that I experienced an everlasting expression of authentic friendship. It happened one night after visiting hours.

The hum of the machine was my only "companion," which

was anything but pleasant. The creak of my hospital door caught my attention, and friendship walked in.

Her name: **Carol**. She and I met when we were in middle school, and a friendship was born. A remarkable relationship of 60 years and still strong. Such can only be called: phenomenal.

Not one to let barriers get in her way, Carol quietly came up to my room by the back staircase. With a gigantic smile, she made herself at home, and the conversation lasted well into the night. I felt so miserable until she joined me after visiting hours, just to see how I was doing. **True friendship at its best.** Her action taught me the genuine value of caring and love.

After three days I left the hospital, very weak and sad for missing so much of the college classes. However, lessons in life arrive in multiplicity, and we either gain insights from them or ignore and deny their face value.

**Whatever your thing is, a true friend likes you,
not despite it—but because that's what makes you, you.**

---Alain de Botton

My Comrade

Another lesson of friendship was awaiting around the corner. As a child, I grew up in southern Georgia in a very quiet and calm town. To me, Fitzgerald was a perfect place to live—the kind of a place where everyone knows almost everyone else. Next door was my best friend; she was born twenty days after I was, so our relationship started out very young. Her name: **Gail.** If one could combine all the positive terms surrounding the true meaning of friendship, you would have a glimpse of who Gail is…to this day. It was indeed a very tragic day when my family had to move away after elementary school. We ended up in Florida, 300 miles from where Gail was, but we were faithful to keep in touch.

While I was recovering from my collapsed lung, Gail convinced her mom to drive the distance to check on my well-being—300 miles just to see if I was doing okay. Their visit was only for a weekend, but I mattered. Such friendship is not measured by a spatial distance. The length of time and space is not even questionable. It didn't even merit a conversation between Gail and her mom about "should we go see him," or "should we just wait" –*"Mom, gas up the car, pack the luggage, and let's head out now."* This is unquestionable, authentic friendship.

CHAPTER 6

The Chasing Waiter

Rene has a contagious laughter that unless you have passed on from this life to the next, you might as well prepare your funny bone to get a workout. I would often meet her for lunch, and on this particular day, we decided to risk eating at a new restaurant down the street from her workplace. A risk? Only because we had heard nothing good or bad about its cuisine.

The meal was palatable, and as always, the topics of conversation between Rene and me were intriguing, with a mixture of uncontrollable laughter and entertainment. Not a care in the world—we resembled two comedians enjoying one another's company. The lunch hour zoomed by. Neither Rene nor I gave attention to the finishing touch of the meal—the tip!

As we were ambling back to Rene's workplace, we heard this screeching noise behind us. Literally running down the sidewalk towards us was our waiter, screaming something in a language that was certainly not English. For a brief moment, I thought he was "speaking in tongues" as some religious folks believe in doing.

Shock was an understatement of the astonishing reaction that Rene and I had. Being chased down the street by an angry waiter definitely was not a normal occurrence that one witnessed in St. Petersburg, Florida. After reaching safety (Rene's cubicle) and after the shock dissolved, we realized that neither of us had left a tip. With friendship comes great laughter which became a reality at that precise moment. And to this date, Rene and I still laugh "our heads off" when we re-live the "angry waiter, no tip, screaming the unknown language" episode.

**Many people will walk in and out of your life,
but only true friends will leave footprints in your heart.**

---Eleanor Roosevelt

I found a confidant who was par excellence in trustworthiness, humility, and wisdom in our relationship. To me, he was a walking giant of a gentleman. At the time I had a prominent position on a church staff. As with all jobs, there will be occasional misunderstandings and hurt feelings, even in a church environment. Just because a setting is labeled a "Christian" organization doesn't mean disagreements and trampled feelings don't happen, since human beings are involved. I personally encountered some traumatic, devastating situations.

Out of the need to vent, I would call my friend, C., and arrange a lunch meeting. We discovered a small restaurant where we knew it would be safe and secure to let it all "hang out" and boy! Did I. We named the restaurant Watergate. So each time I needed to talk, I'd call C. and say, "If you are free for lunch, I'll meet you at the Watergate." He never ever refused to meet.

The purpose of this story is that while we may have a multiplicity of friends, there may be a special confidant. And such is normal and okay. Among all of our friends, we may be fortunate to have one or two confidants besides our significant other. If you do, you are blessed in an extra way. C. and his wife, J., have been my friends for over 33 years, and the friendship is still strong and special.

Good friends are like stars.
You don't always see them,
but you know they're always there.

---unknown

CHAPTER 7

Jacob

Jacob left the party...alone. Not because he wanted to leave, but because he felt disengaged from everyone there. The crowd was huge and the high school graduates were in a festive mood. But not Jacob. He was alone, alone. His entire high school existence was exactly that...existing. At times the loneliness seemed to swallow him. Throughout his four years in high school, he wandered from one party to another, never connecting with any of his classmates.

In reality, he didn't know how. As far back as his memory took him, he had been a loner. He didn't want to be. At times he would make an awkward move to actually connect with someone, boy or girl. It didn't matter to Jacob. He just wanted a friend...someone to talk to, or to go places together, or to simply share in some activity. His world was dark and dreary. As an only child, his parents just didn't fulfill his need for a companion—someone to go hiking with or to the movies, or to walk the mall.

Sadly, he was a recluse-internally. The longing to connect with others was persistent, but the unknown internal fright was a blockade. *"Why am I like this?" "What's wrong with me?"* These questions haunted him all the time. Because there was no connection, he thought it was because he didn't feel worthy to be in any type of relationship. He'd be the first to admit that his opinion of himself was at ground zero or even deeper. Because of his total lack of friends, he didn't consider it worthwhile to even take care of himself: hygiene, orderly attire, or a pleasant appearance. He looked ragged.

Jacob's self-esteem, self-image, and self-worth were practically non-existent. If he had any, it was well camouflaged. At school, classmates passed by him as if he were Casper the Ghost. To them, he just didn't exist.

Football was the major sport at Jacob's award-winning high school. Pep rallies were held on Fridays during the last class of the day. The purpose was for the student body to yell and scream their undying devotion to the football jocks who paraded across the stage. It was the last regular game of the season, and the team would make it to the play-offs. On Friday, the students were ecstatic as they practically ran down the halls to get to the auditorium for a choice seat. The scene of bumping, knocking into each other, running, and jolting the next person resembled wild horses being corralled in a large pen.

Jacob was not in the least interested in the hoopla, and was headed toward the serene quietness of the library. Coming in the opposite direction was the most beautiful girl he had ever laid eyes on. She was heading toward the auditorium. Just as Jacob and she were parallel to each other, the calamity happened.

Running smack into her path was a classmate in a rush to get to the auditorium where the action promised to be phenomenal. The last regular football game of the winning season. The notebook papers of the gorgeous girl flew everywhere in the crowded hallway, her books became like military weapons, and her notebooks looked like NASA missiles.

Jacob bent down to help the attractive classmate pick up the scattered paraphernalia. His heart began suddenly palpitating. His legs felt weak, and he felt his entire body was mildly shaking. His mouth went dry as he looked up at the petite girl, and he murmured, *"Let me help you."* He was mesmerized by her beauty, charm, and friendliness. He found it hard to put a complete sentence together. *"I'm, uh, glad to be of help to you." "What else can I do?"* With a contagious smile, she answered, *"Nothing at all. You have done enough." "But I want to show my appreciation. Are you busy after school today?" "Uh, no, but you don't have to do anything for me."* Her response was quick and sincere. *"Let's meet at Lu Ann's Soda Shop for a treat."*

Trembling with excitement, Jacob was fast on the draw. *"Okay. It's a date. I mean meeting."* With a grin, she replied, *"Okay. By the way, my name is Rose Mary."* As she began to leave, over her shoulder, she said with a grin, *"See you soon."* Jacob was in La

La Land and was clueless as to what happened the rest of the school day.

Jacob began a journey that would take him from obscurity into a "land of meaning and purpose" because of a girl named Rose Mary.

**True friends are never apart,
maybe in distance but never in heart.**

----anonymous

CHAPTER 8

The Neighbor Comrade

They were inseparable. They lived side by side as neighbors for 13 years. He was older than she by several days, so in his masculine mind, he believed that it was his responsibility to watch closely over her. Nothing was ever proclaimed as a duty by the parents, but it was simply a gut feeling with him. Justin's friendship with Julie was on the level of a brother-sister relationship. If they had maturity and ability to put the right words on paper, they could have composed a top selling book on the values of the solid, steady, and enriching components that were melted into their relationship. Where one went, the other tagged along--two comrades bonded together as partners should be.

Saturday afternoons were movie outings. They would split the costs of getting into the picture show, plus buying the popcorn, candy, and drinks. Usually the small community would have cowboy movies on the big screen, and Julie would get "into" such shows as much as Justin would. Living only five blocks away from the movie theater, these two friends would walk briskly back home after the movie, play acting various scenes from the movie. They would hoot and holler all the way, not caring what neighbors would think.

Church life was important in the lives of the two families. Attending church functions was expected of Julie and Justin. They, of course, were quite cooperative about being participants in the church activities that catered to their young age group. The more, the merrier.

What was "dangerous" was when the parents allowed these two friends to sit together during the worship service. It was not unusual for one to share goodies with the other. Candy and bubble gum passed from one person to the other person. Some of the goodies were leftovers from the Saturday movies. Sharing one's wealth of goodies was expected and appreciated.

Besides such sharing, it was indeed rare that Justin and Julie could sit through an entire service without getting tickled about something or poking each other. Human nature "mandated" humorous interactions between the two. They would get a few stern stares from the parents, but such would cause the two buddies to simply accelerate the mischievous acts. Finally, enough was enough, and one of the parents would plant their body between the two bosom friends, thus ending what Julie and Justin thought was a delightful worship service.

As neighbors, it was customary for the twosome to walk or ride their bikes to school. School- prepared lunches did not exist, so Justin and Julie would return to their homes for lunch, or eat the lunches at school that had been prepared by their mothers. They especially loved eating at school together because they could share their meals: Justin hated celery and Julie despised raw carrots, so they would switch.

It was not unusual for them to share answers on homework assignments. Throughout elementary school, they trusted each other with the answers, and it was no surprise that their grades were nearly the same. Academically, they were on the same level, which complemented their relationship.

Then the unthinkable happened—Julie's parents needed to move out of town—a better job, another city, a different state, an abrupt change.

The two were devastated. The shock was traumatic! Their small world crumbled. The acceptance between the two was impossible. And the agony was torturous.

Moving day arrived. All the family's friends were supportive and in attendance, except for Justin, who could not be located. Deep into the forest, behind their homes, walked the missing friend. He was unable to face the event. His tears clouded his path as he stumbled along the way. His sadness and depression were totally unbearable.

Julie didn't have the chance to say goodbye. She was heartbroken as she glanced once more at her deserted house and then at Justin's home. With a steady flow of tears, she curled up in a ball in the back seat and buried herself in her car blanket—the next time she looked out the window, she was long gone from her small community and long gone from Justin, her best friend.

**We secure our friends not by accepting
favors but by doing them.**

----Thucydides

CHAPTER 9

Self-Esteem

A positive self-esteem is a vital ingredient in a valid friendship with others. A high self-esteem gives one self-respect, which is needed in any relationship, because the individual is aware of what he or she is permitted or not in the companionship. We are in charge of our bodies physically, mentally, emotionally, socially, and spiritually. These five components comprise who we are and what we are becoming.

A positive self-esteem allows one to appreciate his or her being and as a result, one can do the same towards others without judging or condemning them. Somewhere in one's life journey, he or she hopefully comes to the acute realization that one has not been given the right or responsibility to judge the character make-up of another human being. Best leave it to God to do the evaluation—Matthew 7:1-3.

All of us are in the state of becoming--a state of growing. A healthy self-esteem motivates the individual to forge ahead and not live in the past. When trauma awaits us, our positive self-esteem encourages all of us to plow through with our heads up. When something traumatic or some hardship come our way, we can use it as a teaching tool in which to learn some of life's lessons. A strong self-esteem can activate one's imagination and creativity in which to learn, to grow, to become.

Friends with a positive self-esteem can usually tell to what degree their comrades rate on the self-esteem level. If the friend has a low opinion of self, the positive thinking pal will want to help build the esteem of the friend. It's going to be a lopsided relationship if there is a distinct difference in the self-esteem category between the two. The goal needs to be helping the low esteem person grow inwardly which in turn changes the outward person. It isn't a fast process because the poor self-esteem individual has to muster up the courage and fortitude to enact the changes. But the friend is there to encourage and to guide. It becomes a privilege, an honor, in which to help someone else. Such is based on a loving, respectful, and trustworthy relationship.

Maintaining a positive self-esteem makes life exciting and livable. The individual has adopted values which he or she centers his or her life around. Decisions, actions, and communication skills all reflect the person's positive character towards self, and in the direction of the many friends he or she has. When they speak, everyone hears and understands the communication from the lips of their friend.

The one with a high self-esteem has the innate courage to speak up and, if need be, will even express one's different opinion from others in a calm, kind, non-defiant way. He has no desire to browbeat anyone, but simply realizes that he or she is just as equal as everyone else in the group. The healthy self-esteem exhibits positive behavior because his and her lives center around their wholesome value system.

In some conversations, there will most likely be a difference of expressed opinions about a subject matter. This is normal. The individual with a positive self-esteem will accept the possible criticism without taking it to heart.

When debate issues come up, the high esteem person doesn't engage in a free-for-all. The positive self-esteem person can stay with the heated debate, but he or she will communicate their likes and dislikes, without feelings of fear and anxiety.

An individual who has a healthy self-esteem does not have to prove himself or herself to anyone. In fact, it is not unusual for such a person to make a constructive difference in the lives of those with low self-esteem. The individual with the high self-esteem usually has no problem accepting people the way they are with unconditional acceptance. In turn, they are the ones who help others gain greater confidence and can lead them in a positive direction to success and greater happiness. As a result, the high self-esteem person has no qualms about developing a loving and respectful relationship with those who are emotionally hurting. The ones with a good self-esteem feel at ease communicating with others because they have confidence in themselves with what they are saying. They can help the other person focus on what can be done to enhance one's poor self-esteem.

The vital thing is that the healthy person values and accepts others to the point of not trying to change them. This is not the responsibility of the healthy friend.

The flip side of the coin are the individuals who suffer from a low self-esteem. Those with low self-esteem are victims. They try to please everyone which turns out to be royal disaster. They live in a world where others attempt to manipulate them, and the low self-esteem has difficulty saying NO because of being a people pleaser. They struggle with inner confidence, so they are at the mercy of others. A low self-esteem places incredible burdens on the person. They have very little confidence and faith in their own opinions, since they have continual doubts about whether their thoughts are good enough to mention. They live within the shadow of the high esteem individual.

Because they tend to doubt their decisions in life, they can have a sense of worthlessness. Trying new activities is a scary risk that they shy away from. Life seems bleak and pessimistic. Their outlook on life is based on their low self-esteem, so life is clouded with negativities. They desire a successful life but since they doubt their abilities and talents, life is an uphill battle. As a result, they will possibly experience frequent emotions of fear, anxiety, and horrible depression.

Due to comparing themselves to others, usually those with a positive self-esteem, they always come in second best or even third or fourth. Their thinking borders on the negative, and their expectations in life are few because they fear failure. When they are complimented for any achievements, they question the validity of the praise. They can actually feel awkward and undeserving of the praise.

There are ways of improving one's self-esteem, and a professional therapist can be the means of doing so.

A true friend never gets in your way unless you happen to be going down.

--Arnold Glasgow

SELF-IMAGE

How one sees himself or herself is determined by one's self-image, and our self-image is directly tied to our self-esteem. A negative self-esteem will produce a low self-image, and a positive self-image stems from a self-esteem that is healthy and wonderful. The way one evaluates his or her idea of self-appearance is one of the ingredients that make up our self-image. Along with our appearance is also our idea of the abilities and type of personality we have. If the idea of our appearance, abilities, and personality is positive, then we will have a healthy self-image. The mental picture we have of ourselves determines the self-image we see.

We have developed our self-image through a learning process. All of our life experiences have helped shape our self-image. If our experiences have mainly been abusive and destructive, then as a result, we see ourselves as damaged material. The joy in life that we might have once had is no longer evident, and our self-image reflects the lack of joy. It is a devastating life in which the self-esteem is also damaged, sometimes beyond repair.

On the flip side of the coin, if an individual has had life fulfilling experiences, a positive self-image is probably intact. The individual can assure himself or herself that one's personality and appearance are pleasable and acceptable in the eyes of self and of society. The positive self-image of the individual takes pleasure in knowing that one's personality traits are positive in nature, perhaps even endearing to others. These positive traits actually define who we are and who we are becoming.

Having a positive self-respect for who we are is essential for a validated self-esteem. If our respect for self is wholesome, it impacts our self-image. No self-respect equals a low level of self-esteem. They go hand-in-hand to produce a mentally healthy person.

As we are growing up, it is one of the responsibilities of our parents to instill in us the importance of a positive self-image. As we mature, we will have the values that accompany a worthy self-image. By doing so, the self-esteem will also be enhanced and positive. We will feel and know that we are of value and of importance to self and to our parents.

On the other hand, if a child is continually bombarded by critical, severe remarks from the parents, the child will be damaged, thus having a damaged self-image with a negative self-esteem. His or her personal view of self will be destructive in nature. It is a very, very sad predicament in which to exist.

The individual with a damaged self-image has such a negative judgment towards his or her internal and external self that life, overall, has a menacing cloud following one's actions and thoughts. It is a terrible way of life. Because of their low self-image, some individuals will attempt to become perfectionists. This goal opens up a full can of worms which will result in disappointments and discouragements. They will strive, strive, and strive, and yet fail, fail, fail. Sadly, they perpetuate their personal unhappiness which can negatively impact their family and social life.

Goal: Positive Self-Image=Positive Self-Esteem
Poor Self-Image=Negative Self-Esteem

Friends can bolster against loneliness,
decrease anxiety, and improve one's physical health.

--Psychology Today

SELF-WORTH

One's perception of his or her self-worth is tied directly into one's self-esteem. Psychologists claim that self-worth and self-esteem mean the same. I separate the two by connecting one's spirituality with self-worth. It is rare to find individuals who do not believe in some sort of higher power than they are. With that in mind, a person's self-worth can be linked to one's spiritual nature.

An individual who has a positive self-esteem and self-image can well accept that his or her Supreme Being sees each one worthy of love and acceptance. When we can accept such, we then can sense our worthiness based on our faith. This worthiness carries with it positive emotions. Even in our toughest situations in life, we know that our Supreme Being has not cancelled out our worthiness. Our state of merit remains intact. Sometimes knowing such is what gets us actually through those moments of conflict. We are thoroughly convinced that we are "spiritual thoroughbreds" in a world of chaos and of stress.

A person having a healthy self-esteem will also have a positive self-image and self-worth.

The opposite side of the coin is the individual who has a horrible sense of self-worth. The person may believe in a Supreme Being but with emotional strings attached. He or she may also believe that their wrongdoings cause their Higher Power to withdraw the worthiness factor. They see themselves as mental and emotional destitute persons—they have lost the love and kindness of their Supreme Being. As a result, the persons will attempt all sorts of tasks to win back the kindness and love. These individuals have a "roller coaster spirituality" with bumps and bruises. Their sense of self-worth is always in jeopardy, which critically impacts their self-esteem and self-image. It is truly a miserable way to live from day-to-day.

Therefore, the formula looks like this:

Healthy self-esteem = positive self-image and self-worth
Unhealthy self-esteem = negative self-image and self-worth

CHAPTER 10

Effective Communication

If a relationship is to grow in a healthy manner, to survive long term, and to maintain its significance, there must be a phenomenal communication system in the friendship. The joy of communication is the opportunity of openly sharing feelings and thoughts about one's life goals and desires.

When we are expressing our desires, goals, thoughts, feelings, and actions, we are being vulnerable since we are opening ourselves up to another person. Communicating effectively removes barriers between the two individuals. Each is hearing what the other is saying rather than playing a guessing game. There are no ambiguities, demands, or "shoulds" in the conversation. Simply put, it is two friends having a conversation based on honesty, openness, and actually entertaining at times.

Positive, effective communication between friends **cannot** be accomplished by one person doing all the talking while the other individual is not given the opportunity to respond. Such communication is a dead-end avenue. It goes nowhere. When transacted meaningfully, communication allows a special bonding that may not happen in any other means. In a relationship, positive communication is crucial if the partnership is going to endure in a loving and caring way.

Every individual needs someone in his or her life who will listen, listen, listen. Whether it is just wanting to pass the time or bare one's soul, we want to have an audience of at least one person. In such a situation, having a friend is a true blessing. So many times, we are interrupted in our thinking process with speculations and unsolicited advice-giving from the other person. Rather than listening to what we have to say, we are cut off at the pass by someone who does not have the patience or desire to listen to all that we have to say.

Each person is worthy of respect and attention while he or she is talking. All of us deserve ample time to complete our thoughts with undivided attention. Who knows? One may actually learn something new by simply listening. Each person is a teacher, in a way, when sharing knowledge or personal revelations to a friend. This becomes a valuable gift that is freely bestowed to a special friend. What a tremendous blessing it can turn out to be.

However, for the blessing to take place, we have to focus on what our friend is sharing. If we permit our mind to wander into LaLa Land, we will miss out on the communication. Attentive listening is essential! Sometimes we make the error in having a response before our friend is finished talking. Our friend may be expressing deep "gut" feelings, and he or she needs our full listening attention without our interruption. We need to allow them to express the full essence of what they are thinking and feeling.

Friendship is a sheltering tree.

---Samuel Coleridge

As a clinical therapist, my attention has to be given to what the person is communicating and even not communicating. There are stories that break my heart, and as best as I know how, I show them a boat load of empathy. Often during the sessions with my clients, they are not wanting my advice but simply for me to just listen. And more times than not, through their self-talk, they can solve their problem. I'm there as a facilitator, which is fine with me. The same holds true in a friendship. Listening with genuine empathy enhances the relationship.

When a friend places oneself into the shoes of the other person, the individual can sense what his or her friend is talking about. What a tremendous feeling it becomes. It is so much easier to empathize with what is being communicated. A valid connection is born.

When I was working on my master's degree in clinical therapy, my professors drilled into us the dynamics of attentive listening.

49

We were instructed to observe the client's body language, facial expressions, and for certain, maintain eye contact. In addition, we were to repeat to the individual the key points of what was expressed.

When we have "the floor" and are free to communicate our feelings, we need to pause long enough for our listening partner to respond. He or she may actually say something we haven't thought about—that is, if we give the individual the opportunity to talk.

This is a must!

Before we involve others in a serious conversation, we need to set our boundary with them. Do we just want to vent without any feedback, or do we seek out our friend's opinion? Before we begin "spilling our gut" to the friend, establishing our boundary is essential or a volcanic explosion can occur.

To ensure an effective communication, select a place where very few distractions are likely to occur. Don't risk getting bombarded with distractions, such as traffic, loud noises, or friends making an appearance. If distractions are certain to happen, why meet in the first place? Neither person is going to feel heard or understood. More than likely it will turn out to be a royal farce.

What really matters when we are talking is that the person(s) is giving us the full attention we deserve. We can usually tell if the listener is daydreaming or waiting to pounce on us with unsolicited advice.

Effective and empathetical communication is a dynamic ingredient in a friendship. It bonds, solidifies, and enhances the relationship in a marvelous way.

Friends are those rare people who ask how you are and then wait to hear the answer.

---Ed Cunningham

CHAPTER 11

Loneliness

One would never think that loneliness was becoming an epidemic, but it is. We usually associate "epidemic" with a disease, not a mental disorder. An individual afflicted with loneliness has several symptoms that are common in nature. One is that an individual suffering from loneliness may claim not to be a social person, thus isolating oneself from others. Being alone may not feel awkward or even strange but rather quite normal and commonplace. Loneliness can prevail.

Another symptom is that the individual has difficulty even reaching out to others, with the express purpose of not making new friends. A true tragedy. There seems to be a gigantic barrier that is impossible to penetrate. Individuals with the "loneliness" factor are good at not being social and are not comfortable making new friends.

Fortunately, loneliness can be dealt with effectively, but such healing does require time, effort, and commitment. The first requirement is that the person needs to receive professional help. Connecting with others is a basic need, and there might just be deep-seated feelings that are causing them to put up a barrier. Face-to-face listening on the part of the individual and the professional is of utmost importance. It is important for the professional to hear the feelings and thoughts of the lonely person in order to help the person have a more enriching life. The feelings are based on one's emotions while the thoughts deal with a person's thought processing. Both are important for the professional to hear. The professional can use one's thoughts and feelings and direct us out of the loneliness syndrome into a richer and fuller life.

One of the most devastating feelings we experience is that of loneliness. When we are experiencing loneliness mentally, we can emotionally feel it. Because of our computer world, plus our mobile devices, we set ourselves up for the loneliness that can happen. We often get lost in the technical devices we use for most of our communications. Much of our world of communicating is now done online. We become totally trapped by the devices which promote the feeling of loneliness. We become absent from person-to-person contact. All of us are susceptible to loneliness. The effects of loneliness can be dangerous and destructive when it is ignored. Our feeling of loneliness needs our attention—our full focus.

Approximately 60 million people in the U. S., or 20% of the total population, feel lonely.

---Dr. John Cacioppo
University of Chicago

According to medical research, the power of loneliness can have a negative impact on our cardiovascular system and on our immune resources. There is also a link between loneliness and depressive episodes. It is not uncommon for the individual to experience insomnia, which causes a problem in daily functioning at work and at home. As if these weren't bad enough, there is the risk factor of suicide, stemming from one's depression. The individual suffering from loneliness can become pessimistic in every aspect of life.

The lonely person also faces an increased risk of a stroke, high blood pressure, and even weight gain. Perhaps we have underestimated the psychological and physiological damage that loneliness can do to the human body. Our naivety, to some degree, has been a serious detriment in our comprehension of the dynamics involved in loneliness.

Loneliness can cause us to withdraw from our friends and into ourselves. We seclude ourselves from society and become much like hermits. Furthermore, the longer we are in the withdrawn state, the worse it can become. We can get to the point in which we no longer acknowledge our friends and sadly, vice versa.

It is true that our friends can enable us to be involved in each other's goals, successes, and amusements. Research has proven that when our stress level is lessened, serious loneliness can be kept at bay, our bodies are healthier, and longevity is enhanced when we have friends who love us and care about our well-being.

One way to combat the sense of loneliness is to take the risk of opening oneself up to people. The conversation can occur at work, school, church, and yes, even in the supermarket grocery line. Even when you are not in a state of loneliness, open up to people, even strangers, in a cordial way. You will feel better, and you might brighten the day of another person. It feels good to communicate ideas, dreams, goals, and even mundane information with others, and in turn, hear what others have to say. As human beings, we desire and need a connection and communication with others. Perhaps we, in our society, have become reluctant, even somewhat frightened, to open up to others. Have you?

The mystery is that we may have a sense of loneliness even when surrounded by a crowd of people. We can't quite figure out the reason. We just do. There are several reasons we may feel the sad feeling of loneliness. If an individual suffers from depression or clinical anxiety, then he or she can feel the impact of desolation--pure loneliness. Mixing depression and anxiety with loneliness can produce an extremely sad and forsaken person.

Another reason for loneliness is when the individual, for whatever reason, has withdrawn from his or her social circle. The person is left totally destitute in an extroverted society.

Furthermore, one can feel lonely when a tragedy has taken place, like a divorce, a significant death, moving away from home, or any other disruptive event that has plagued us.

It is rare that one's loneliness is created by one single cause. Since this state of mind is unique to each individual, the causes and overall treatment will vary. The degree to which a person feels alone and possibly unwanted depends on many varied factors, but the common line is a horrible feeling of emptiness. It is a miserable emotion.

Individuals suffering from a low self-esteem can actually feel unwanted, useless, and unworthy of love and attention, thus inviting loneliness into their lives. Loneliness brings horrible negative effects into one's life, thus producing possible clinical depression.

One of the solutions of loneliness is additional social interaction than one may currently have. Force yourself to go to where people are congregating. You don't necessarily have to know them. A grocery store, a mall, a church, or a social event can all be wonderful resources to experience some social interactions that will combat the loneliness that you might feel at the time. Associating socially with others through civic clubs, religious organizations, friends, and family members can help a lonely person emerge out of his or her cocoon into the sunshine of socialization with others.

Since 1985, the number of people in the U. S. with no close friends has tripled.

---www.verywellmind.com

Being a clinical therapist, my first suggestion, of course, is to recommend therapy. Talking out one's thoughts and feelings can reveal the reasoning behind one's social isolation. You can learn how to connect effectively with others. Talking with one's therapist can open the floodgates of insights, concrete ideas, and possibilities. It may be that the therapist will want you to participate in group therapy. It isn't scary! By doing so, a support system is established which can be a positive in one's life. It connects you with others who are experiencing the same trauma. It does a person good to know that he or she is not alone in the sinking canoe.

I consider my three cats and three dogs as my means of escaping out of loneliness into a healthier well-being state. They can cause me to laugh out loud and step outside of my lonely self into taking care of their needs of food, shelter, and love. They are amazing pets that "minister" to my needs. Other pets may offer the same, and it is called <u>pet therapy.</u>

Loneliness can be a thing of the past. But it does have a requirement: the person has got to want to change. Overcoming loneliness can begin in a simple way: **begin by making contact with individuals who have the same interests.** In such situations, friendships can develop and flourish. The more a person becomes involved with others, the more likely friendships will develop, and loneliness will lessen. Wonderful social relationships can emerge, and a genuine respect for one another will develop. This can be the beginning of a long-term relationship.

The formula for escaping loneliness is done best in "baby steps" rather than in gigantic leaps. At first, join just one community or church function and explore it. Then later on, another one. Loneliness can be conquered. It simply takes will-power and commitment. Try it and see.

CHAPTER 12

Life Happens

Even in the best relationship, there may be times when misunderstandings occur. Hurt feelings can happen. It's called **human nature**. It certainly does not have to be the end of the friendship. When the situation happens, usually both parties experience sad, bad feelings and thoughts. Each one can actually believe that they have been wronged and that it's not his or her fault. These are normal reactions.

We can make matters worse by waiting for the other person to bury the hatchet and apologize. The longer the stand-off lasts, the worse matters can become. The fire in our mental furnace blazes, and the relationship suffers in a desperate manner. If the truth be known, both parties are miserable. The unhappiness permeates their souls and causes terrible heartache. They long to be together again—to enjoy the private talks, the laughter, and the excursions—just being together. The truth is that the one who comes forth to make things right is the stronger of the two.

It requires integrity and inner strength to swallow one's pride in order for the relationship to be restored and healed.

A break-up in the relationship doesn't mean that the friendship was flawed in the beginning. Fractures happen due to misunderstandings or miscommunications. In reality, both friends have very uncomfortable feelings—they truly miss one another. They are miserable and extremely sad. They feel disconnected, and it is a gut-wrenching, destitute feeling. Not an easy emotion to wrestle with. As the adage goes: **life happens.** It isn't a hopeless act when the relationship turns sour for a period of time. In most authentic relationships, the two individuals are hoping to repair the friendship, and due to their desire and willingness, the relationship can be restored in order that they can forgive each other and move on. It is like a breath of fresh, clean air.

When the relationship is revived, the individuals are on fabulous terms once again, and the repair work was totally successful. When a break-up has occurred with a significant individual, we have a longing to make things right. We want the relationship restored. Once the friendship is put together again, the cloud of despair disappears, whatever apparent guilt is buried, and the atmosphere is bright, sunny, and refreshing.

Forgiveness with both individuals has to occur if the relationship is to be reinstated. It really isn't all that difficult once one puts aside his or her pride. The joining together again becomes a joyous occasion. Hugs, smiles, handshakes all become overt signs of forgiveness and genuine friendship.

If we are to forgive, we need a tolerance of others as generous as that tolerance we display toward our own errors.

---Friendship Factor

Because forgiveness is such a strong, positive force, it binds tightly the two friends. One can actually feel the dynamics of the act of forgiveness. It is an awesome feeling that can send chills throughout one's body. Since forgiveness can cause such positive feelings, each friend is on the receiving line of love and kindness. What a remarkable act of a true friendship.

The relationship becomes a joy again. Each person takes immense pleasure watching the other live his or her life, reaching goals and experiencing successes. It is important to talk freely about one's feelings of what happened. This is not to be an accusing session! It's to be a time when two friends can share their feelings about the misunderstanding in a loving, caring, and healthy way.

It's important to allow each person to complete their thoughts without any interruptions. The responsibility of the other person is to listen attentively until it's her or his turn to communicate one's thoughts and feelings. The most profound compliment one can give to the other is to listen, listen, listen to what the person is communicating. Being a good listener builds a relationship that can be everlasting.

CHAPTER 13

Testimonies of Friendship

I met my dear friend of 64 years at the age of 10. We have been through a lot together. We went through part of elementary school, junior high school, and senior high school at the same time. She was from an upscale family, which I was not. She didn't care. We formed a bond that hasn't been broken to this day.

I was raised in a Methodist church while she was in a Baptist church. One time she took me to her Baptist youth group, and I totally enjoyed it. That is where I became saved and baptized into the Baptist faith.

She went with me through some horrible life situations. I went through an accidental death of her husband with her.

Later in life we both remarried to wonderful Christian men. But her husband is now suffering with terminal cancer and mine with end-stage Alzheimer's disease.

We are on the phone constantly, holding each other up as we go through the struggles we are now facing. One thing is for sure: our friendship has remained intact all these years and continues even to this day.

Betty Noble Card

Life Saver
It is with great humility that I place this testimony in this book.

It has been 28 years ago that I first met Dr. Ray Ashurst. I had some issues that needed dealing with that had happened to me much of my life. I went to visit Dr. Ashurst, not knowing what to expect. Much to my surprise, by the end of that first meeting, I had become very comfortable with him and made a second appointment. This started a very long process in which not only was he a clinical therapist, but he became a friend. This made things so much easier to open up to him and start my understanding of my feelings and events that had happened to me, and the healing process began. Through this long process of appointments, I learned a great deal that was really mind-blowing, not only about what had happened to me but that I was worth something. I saw Dr. Ashurst sometimes 2 or 3 times a week for the first bit and then once a week. I know that there were several times that I had called between 12 AM and 3AM, only to be told, "I will have the lights on, so come on over." Never once did he tell me, "No, you can't come. It's after hours." He would talk to my son when my son would see him and would answer any questions that my 5-year old asked and would explain things to him in a way that his mind could understand. This gave me more confidence in Dr. Ashurst as a therapist and as a friend. There is no way that I can put into words how this man helped my son and me. I can tell you this though: if it were not for God putting Ray in our lives, I have no idea where I would be now. Ray walked me through the toughest things in my life that NO ONE should ever have to go through. I thank God for putting this man in my path and for giving him the knowledge of how to help my son and me. Through the years, I have always been able to call and to talk with him about things going on in my life. God gave me a life saver when I was sinking and needed a human to physically sit, talk, listen, help, and give me advice. Thank you so much, Ray, for always being there. You are truly a blessing.

---Lori Copeland

Recently I was asked
"What is the difference between love and being in love?"
This question deserved great thought.
I wasn't clear about how I viewed the two
Or had I even considered them separate.
This is what I came up with for myself.
Love is: when someone touches my heart
Being in love: When someone touches my soul.

---Helen Kirk

MY BEST FRIEND SHILOH

I recently lost my best friend through kidney disease. She left this earth with love and dignity. We had a friendship for twelve years. We had so much fun together, and she made me laugh even when I was down. We would get a wild streak, put on classic rock and dance all over the house.

We went on rides just to see what we would find. We watched movies and ate popcorn. Her favorite was watermelon. The girl could eat a ton of it! She was so intuitive. I'm a diabetic, and she somehow knew when my sugar was high. She let me know, and she was always right.

We were two peas in a pod. My friend just sat and listened when I dumped all my problems of the day on her. She was such a good egg and sat quietly and listened. She was such a loyal friend. I knew she would never spread rumors or hurt me like others had done.

I guess I should let the reader of this story know that my best friend was a Boxer dog named Shiloh. She was my everything and a gift. The people who gave her to me as an infant had no idea what she would become to me.

She was the runt of the litter, and her mother didn't want to care for her. So, she was bottle-fed, and she had a big will to live. She was a wiggly, happy, loving dog. She made me laugh every day with all her antics. It was also her job to protect me, and she was very serious about that job.

Shiloh sat with me in my double chair every night with her head on my lap. I miss that most of all. The night before she was put to sleep, it was like she knew. She cuddled with me all night. At one point, she put her muzzle on my face and left it there a long time. I knew she was telling me goodbye, and it was like she was saying Thank You for loving me so much.

---Debbie Pannell

CHAPTER 14

Sarah and Her Loneliness

She lived all alone. She was a loner. Her loneliness was totally unbearable. The nights were all consuming. No one was part of her solitary world. Life seemed unforgiving and very desolate. The nights seemed darker than dark and deeply morose. Her days were horribly grotesque and depressive. Her life was simply mentally and emotionally empty. There was no order to her life—no logic, no nothing. Her existence was a complete blah. Such as her life had been for more years than her memory could possibly recall. One day seemed exactly like the other.

There was once a time many years ago, when Sarah's life was drastically different: parties, teas, shopping, friendship, family, laughter, and trips. But everything had become extinct due to age and gradual changes. Such were things in the life of the aged woman. Counting her end days was not unusual for the tired, old lady. Maybe her death would happen soon, she hoped...maybe tomorrow was her wish.

Before his reformation, Christmas Scrooge had a more

exciting life than Sarah, the tired, decrepit octogenarian. Her days seemed so long, the nights longer, and life seemed senseless, without meaning. Eighty years, plus, on earth, and life was futile, miserable, and without purpose.

Sarah had been living in Northeast Georgia for 20 years. During the winter months, the temperatures could chill one's bones. Mix it with a brisk wind, and you realized that a warm, comfortable home was a necessity. On a particular night in February, such was the case of Sarah. She wrapped herself around with an electric lap blanket, a beautiful blazing fire in the hearth, and her home was toasty warm. She was deeply involved in a mystery novel when a scratching at her front door startled her.

"What in the world?"

Sarah rose gingerly from her comfy lazy-boy chair. When she opened the squeaky door, she gasped, mouth wide open.

Staring at her was a brown, black, white, and filthy dirty German Shepherd. Shaking from head to toe, the visitor was freezing.

"Get lost, you mongrel. Go!!"

The visitor did not move a muscle, her eyes were focused on Sarah, never wavering. Her brown eyes were glued to the old woman.

"Go!"

Since German Shepherds are known for their stubborn behavior, this one was definitely no exception.

"I said for you to get lost, you mutt."

The visitor moved rather slowly towards Sarah, her eyes fixated on the owner of the warm, inviting home.

"Good grief. Ok, come on in for a minute, and that's all."

The Shepherd wagged its tail like a pendulum and made her way cautiously into the home.

"You are a mess. I'll get a towel to wipe you down and some
left-overs, but tomorrow you are out of here. You hear?"

Sleepy time arrived. Sarah headed to her bedroom, and the visitor settled in front of the fireplace. The lights were turned off for a long winter's night.

During the night, it happened! Sarah was brought out of a deep, comfortable sleep by a cold nose against her facial cheek. Up and at 'em, Sarah was ready to battle whatever it was.

When she opened her wide eyes, she came face-to-face with her visitor.

"Good stars, stop licking my face with your sloppy tongue."

This demand only stirred the Shepherd more: sloppy, sloppy, sloppy.

"You are a crazy rascal. That's what I'll call you: Rascal."

Without warning, Rascal gave Sarah a wet kiss on the lips.

"Yuck!"

When Sarah awoke the following morning, Rascal had established residence on Sarah's bed.

"Oh brother."

As the morning moved into the afternoon, Sarah had forgotten her threat to turn the visitor out into the snow. Instead, Sarah could sense Rascal's need to go for a walk. After all, Rascal had gradually become a "house partner" in just a few hours. Sarah dressed warmly and out they went—their first walk together. Sarah had no idea what would happen...an aged woman with a frisky German Shepherd.

"What am I gonna do about you?"

Rascal's ears stood erect as if she knew exactly what the question was. She nuzzled even closer to Sarah as they made their journey. Neither seemed fully aware of the cold temperature or brisk wind, or even the beautiful snowflakes gently falling to the cold ground.

As they strolled down the country road, Sarah recognized one of her neighbors walking towards them. Rascal knew instinctively to position herself between Sarah and the neighbor. Rascal was definitely a "watch dog" --protecting her cranky-old master.

They greeted one another briefly and continued on their journey. The farther they walked, the more neighbors they encountered, and the more individuals they met, the nicer and more comfortable Sarah became with their personalities.

"What a nice neighborhood," she told her new four-legged friend.

Sarah began to feel a warm change of feeling about her neighbors—she hadn't felt that way in quite a few years.

Eventually Sarah and Rascal found themselves back at home.

On that day, Sarah's neighborhood seemed smaller, people became friendlier, and her life felt lighter and brighter...and as for Rascal—she became a permanent place in Sarah's heart.

CHAPTER 15

God-Sent

I believe that friendships are sent to us by God. I don't think that relationships are just happenstance. My belief is that God brings people together for a purpose. As a reader, you may find this a farfetched concept, which is fine. However, in my case, I see my relationships in a spiritual light. Each person contributes a specific purpose in my life. It may be for entertainment, support, or ego-boosting. The individual is a dynamic factor in my well-being.

There is no question that life for all of us is filled with unbearable stress and heartaches at times. Beyond any shadow of a doubt, life circumstances can be a huge challenge—on a good day. On a bad day, some situations are totally overwhelming—sometimes defeating.

If I felt that I was totally alone, in a spiritual sense, without any divine presence, the depression would be devastating. Many individuals with whom I deal do believe in a "higher power." Whatever one specifies as God, a solid belief that one is under His watchful care in regards to bringing particular individuals into your daily life can be uplifting and comforting.

So, the question is, what is God's purpose for bringing two individuals or more into a dynamic relationship? First of all, there is a wonderful magical connection within the relationship. Whether it involves only one person or more, the magic is present. It's as if one can read the thoughts of the other, or can feel what is going on, or even predict the actual behavior of the friend. The dynamics are vivid and vibrant. It is a marvelous relationship.

**Each friend represents a world in us, a world
possibly not born until they arrive,
and it is only by this meeting that a new world is born.**

---Anais Nin

Secondly, even if you have a special someone from the early grade of kindergarten (like I do), I believe God's hand brought you together. It was as if a magnet drew you together and has kept you in contact all the years since.

Relationships have a spiritual side in them even for those who believe otherwise. Because a friendship is so involved, one's soul and heart are vital ingredients in the relationship. Our very depths interact with those of another. Two (or more) individuals take the risk of being vulnerable and trusting of one another. One's spirituality is not to be ashamed of, embarrassed about, or hidden. It is a vital part of who we are.

When our friend is having some life difficulties, at times we tell him or her that we will remember the person in our prayers. At such point, we have involved God. He is not a foreign being. He makes up our personal spirituality.

Friendships don't just happen as mentioned before. There is a "magnetic pull" that connects one with others. Have you considered that your Supreme Being "delivered" special individuals into your life? As said before, I just don't believe it was happenstance. This author firmly believes God, in His infinite wisdom, knew that I would need certain specific individuals in my life for support, entertainment, and guidance....and I am glad that He did.

Chapter 16

Toxic Relationships

When we hear of specific foods that are toxic in nature, we avoid them like the plague. We know what toxicity will do to our bodies, so we don't take the risk. Nothing can taste that scrumptious to place immediate harm into our lives. The same rationale should be carried over into our relationships. Toxic individuals do not belong in our circle of friendships. They are extremely dangerous!

At moments life can become very difficult to manage. It's at these times we need a genuine friend who will be by our side to support us. We need their encouragement and unconditional love to help guide us through the perplexing situations. The very last element we need is a toxic individual to be in the middle of our difficulties.

Because a toxic person lives in a narcissistic world, he or she has an inflated sense of self-importance. Every aspect of the person's life centers solely around self. Their world is microscopic and to reach out to others without any strings attached is improbable. They stretch out their arms to others with specific strings attached.

One prominent string is to control the lives of others. Since toxic individuals are full-blown controllers, their powerful desires and motives center around being extremely dominate towards others.

Another attached string of toxic people is to get their acquaintances to be totally dependent on them. They might even tell lies to convince others that they need desperately to have them in their arena. It may be a well thought-out gimmick, and toxic people are experts of deception and abusive antics.

Still another dangerous string is the conditional love they place in the relationship. There is usually a suspicious motive behind their so-called love attachment. When the innocent individual hesitates on becoming involved in such a toxic relationship, the malignant individual can become cruel, abusive, and angry. It is not a pretty sight to behold. The venomous individual has no qualms about gossiping and criticizing other innocent people. The truth is insignificant to the toxic person. However, getting a lot of attention feeds their starving ego. Remember, the world's attention has to center around their arena.

Negativity, negativity, negativity—the watchword of a lethal person. When one is dealing with monumental hardships, toxic persons are on hand to judge and to be downright mean through their sarcastic remarks. They have to put their two cents worth into the conversation, and it's usually negative— sometimes even cruel. Don't expect genuine compassion from them about your difficulties. They can be ice cold.

Because toxic people are in a continual state of raw drama,

their goal is to involve individuals who are innocently minding their own business. The toxic person seems always to be in the midst of a "human bullfight"--drama after drama, and they want innocent people to choose sides.

When someone lives in a narcissistic/entitled arena, he or she truly believes the words coming from their mouths are divine. They really aren't interested in listening to what the "commoners" of this world have to say. To the toxic individual, the "commoners" are highly privileged to be part of the listening audience. After all, the toxic person needs to be right, and if it hurts you, that's just too bad. You will get over it in future time, according to the lethal person.

**Some people move our souls to dance
and stay in our hearts forever.**

---Anonymous

God never promised us a life of being surrounded solely by upbeat, optimistic individuals. People who are toxic in nature will make their nasty presence known from time-to-time. Whether it's a male or female, his or her presence will take place.

A toxic male will seek to manipulate our thoughts, emotions, and actions to his way of biased thinking. We can become victims of his way of cognitive behavior, and we lose our true identity. In addition, the male demonstrates a feeling of patronizing superiority due to his ego-driven personality. Over a period of time, we become entangled into a world of toxicity—belligerent, pessimistic, abusive. We hardly recognize ourselves any longer, and our friends begin to peel off. Because of the overbearing personality of the domineering toxic males, they are destructive to be around.

It is one of the blessings of old friends that you can afford to be stupid with them.

---Ralph Waldo Emerson

Toxic women share some of the identical characteristics of the toxic male. Being manipulative is at the top of the list. A toxic woman places full toxic energy into keeping us engaged in the relationship because the toxicity has driven away her friends who once enjoyed being with her. In addition, their jealous streak tends to suffocate all those in the relationship. These friends are not allowed to have other close friends in the arena of the toxic individual. To maintain those in her relationship circle, the toxic person will pull a self-pity show and an over-dramatic demonstration. Great acts for a Hollywood entertainment spectacle. What a hallelujah performance.

If a friend begins to separate from the toxic person, the dangerous individual will possibly use conniving means to conspire against the non-toxic friend through backstabbing and by maligning personality traits of the innocent individual. Toxicity can be contagious. While ruling a person's life, the toxic individual can manipulate the innocent person to the same level as the toxic person and eventually turn the non-toxic individual into a full-blown toxic monster.

Situations do exist within families, in the working environment, among church members, and within social circles that will keep a person tangled up among toxic individuals. It seems at times that there just doesn't seem to be an exit from such vile personalities. Therefore, it is necessary to learn how to handle the toxic people who are a part of one's environment.

People inspire you, or they drain you—pick them wisely.

---Hans F. Hansen

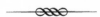

**Just like the toxic male, the toxic female
can be very, very dangerous!**

Self-pitying syndrome is a part of all toxic people who blame everyone but themselves for their miserable lives. *"Woe is me"* all the time. Rather than being sucked into their never-ending drama, one has to vigorously avoid them, along with their self-pitying stages.

Toxic people are narcissistic in nature and believe that the whole realm of their relationships should center around their needs and gratifications. So as to not get caught in such a maze of delusions, the non-toxic person has to completely ignore the toxic, narcissistic person. When one sees them coming in our direction, head out into another direction and don't look back. It isn't a matter of being rude, but rather a matter of not being exposed to the "walking monster" and becoming a victim.

**Life is partly what we make it,
and partly what it is made by the friends whom we choose.**

----Tehyi Hsieh

Someone has said that the only difference between a toxic person and a vulture is that the vulture at least waits until its victim is dead before it begins its attack. Anyone who is doing anything positive will have critics. The truth is that there are toxic individuals who seem to thrive on judging and criticizing others.

Such persons are not going to grow in a positive way until they stop their critical behavior towards others.

Spiritually-speaking, we have never been given the right to downgrade and judge another person. God does the judging because He alone has all the facts regarding the behavior of each person. We are not capable of sitting in judgment against someone else, so we are to keep our mouths closed and our mental attitudes pure—and this is far easier said than done.

Some individuals seem to enjoy hearing and spreading vile comments about someone at work, at church, in our family, or in our social sphere. A boy and his father, with their donkey, were walking through three villages. In the first village, the boy rode the donkey, and the man walked. The people criticized the boy for making his old father walk, and so when they came to the second village, the man rode and the boy walked, and the people in the village criticized the man for making the boy walk. So, they came to the third village, and they both walked and led the donkey. They were both criticized by the people of the village because they did not take full advantage of the donkey's strength. The point of this story is that nobody can please everyone, and toxic so-called "friends" will attack and attack.

Is there a way to erase harmful people from your celebration of life? The answer is yes! One method of steering away from toxic individuals is to associate totally with optimistic friends who have proven their trustworthiness. They have proven to be devoted with no strings attached, their honesty is a guide word, they have a never-ending faith in the relationship, and they are as reliable as one can possibly be.

In order to keep from getting into a relationship with toxic individuals, one has to be continually aware of one's choices of friendships. To have a relationship that lasts through thick and thin requires being in an honest, respectful, genuine relationship of unconditional love and with absolutely no strings attached.

CHAPTER 17

Becoming

All of us are in a state of "becoming"--either we are growing mentally, emotionally, and spirituality, or we are backing up and retrogressing. One thing for certain is that there is no status quo. No one stands still, even though there are those who believe that they are. It is a strong myth.

Solid friendships promote each other "becoming" one's best whether it involves the job one has, or one's personal growth. Friends become cheerleaders to one another —it doesn't stop. It is a continual progression. We may often hear, "I've got your back." When one makes such a commitment, it is like a breath of fresh air. The promise carries elements of love, integrity, security, and safety.

A friend becomes excited and joyful when one's friend is becoming successful. Whether it's the friend reaching a personal goal or emotionally overcoming a heartache, the bottom line is that the individual is becoming victorious. In such a relationship, "becoming" is not to be taken for granted or lightly. It is a vital ingredient in the friendship.

For the individual who is in the midst of the positive aspect of "becoming" as a goal, one's self-esteem, self-worth, and self-image are deeply enhanced. The individual actually can feel the quality and value of the improvement. It is a glorious feeling that can impact one's mental processing, behavioral actions, and spiritual growth. Such is not left to chance, but rather is a reality.

As one lives in a daily perpetual state of "becoming," one can recognize with amazement and breath-taking wonderment the awesome positive change towards others and within oneself. In turn, other individuals will also notice the change and may even express to you the positive difference that they see in you.

Since self-esteem, self-image, and self-worth are interlocked, a person's positive steps of "becoming" will build up the person into tremendous mental and emotional heights. The individual will accomplish worthwhile goals, and such achievements will give uplifting motivation as he or she seeks out additional goals and successes.

In close relationships, the involved individuals must be committed to promoting each other to become one's best if the friendship is to remain valid and intact. It is a matter of giving one another positive, regular "pats on the back" reassurances. Anything less than that will eventually annihilate the relationship, and it will become a faint memory.

Sadly, there can be persons in our circle of relationships

who are "becoming" worse from day-to-day, month-to-month. There is no status quo—each of us is either progressing forward or moving slowly backwards. No matter how hard we try, we cannot make someone step forward in life. We can certainly encourage the individual to develop higher goals, standards, and self-achievements, but to do so rests on the shoulders of each individual.

It's difficult being associated with someone who is a "downer"--a negative, pessimistic person whose whole persona reeks with severe gloominess. His or her life seems dark and almost frightening. The person's overall attitude is based on the premise that the "bad" far outweighs the "good" in life, and the person honestly believes that the bad things will take place more often than the positive situations.

Reprove your friends in secret,
Praise them openly.

---Publilius Syrus

Because such individuals are destructive to be around, it takes a Herculean effort to remain in their presence. Doomsday is always around the corner, and such a negative outlook tends to drag down those around them, including their family members. Since the negative "becomer" already doubts his or her opportunities of successes in life, the individual can have a downward impact on others at work and in social gatherings. It's like inviting the flu to accompany you to these places where a group is gathering. These individuals are contagious. Such a person who is sliding backwards in life situations has little or no emotional positive growth. They are blobs who sadly enough attempt to infiltrate the positive lives of others.

When a person is "busy" in the process of "becoming" on the down slide, he or she perpetuates the attitude of *"Woe is me! Nothing is going to work out for me anyway. So, why try?"* The individuals see themselves as failures, so what's the use in trying anything new? This destructive attitude denotes one's self-esteem, self-worth, and self-image. When all three of these have holes punched in them, the outcome will usually be grotesque.

When any one of us happens to come upon an idea that we think is beneficial and doable for others, we feel elated and proud. Then, along comes Mr. or Ms. Pessimism. Due to perhaps envy or jealousy, this individual rains violently on our super parade. Our dreams and goals can be shot to pieces, along with our ego. They have sucked the progressive breath out of our optimism and self-esteem. It is not a pretty picture. The fresh and healthy air of optimism and of enhancing ideas and goals at the time can be sucked out and through the vents of pessimism, poor self-esteem, with envy and jealousy as sidekicks come sneaking in.

The question is, of course, why does a positive "become" associate with a person who is the opposite? In some situations, there may not be a choice: family relationships and work circumstances are examples. Life-long relationships can also be a reason. There may be a long-lasting bond that involves past personal experiences. Whatever the reason, the perpetual challenge is learning how to mentally and to emotionally stay above the pessimist's lifestyle. This is <u>not</u> going to be an easy task and may even feel impossible at times. However, with perseverance and support from optimistic friends, it is possible.

It is vitally important to remember that remaining in the state of a positive "becoming" individual, a person must keep one's eyes on his or her goals, promote one's boundaries, and be proud of one's achievements.

CHAPTER 18

Mindfulness

Have you ever been in a conversation with a friend, and your mind begins to take a much needed vacation? Your friend is telling you a good story, and part of you is in beautiful Hawaii, exciting New York, or gorgeous Georgia. All of a sudden you hear, *"Well, what do you think?"*

Oh my! You are caught, and you try your best to come up with an innocuous comment as if you have been hanging on his or her every portion of the conversation. Who hasn't been in such a predicament? It isn't that the person's conversation is boring or too mundane, but is simply a matter of human nature. We've been caught not being mindful of what was going on in our presence.

Mindfulness is maintaining who is presently in our personal arena. An awareness, minute-by-minute of paying attention to what is happening around us. A friend has entered our protected arena and by doing so is asking for our full attention. Mindfulness is when we are complying. Our mind may be tempted to wander the wide open spaces. However, we do have the ability and capacity to reign it in.

If we aren't careful, we stop mentally and emotionally being in the present, and we begin "playing in the past" or "rehearsing" for the future. We use up so much of our valuable time in the past or in our future. The last time I personally checked, there is <u>not</u> one thing we can do to undo our past experiences. Whether good or devastating, the past is gone—kaput. You and I can certainly learn from the good or bad of past situations. However, to allow our thoughts and emotions to homestead a location in our past is not only a waste of time, but a loss of our energy.

Life can seem short
Create the moments
You wouldn't mind reliving.

----Helen Kirk

Furthermore, if our minds aren't roaming our past, and we aren't in the here-and-now, then we are preoccupied with the future. We become mentally obsessed with demands, promises, and expectations of tomorrow. Even though we may realize that the day after today is a promissory note, we still take the risk of living tomorrow today. We imagine all sorts of situations, bad or good, about tomorrow and the day after that and the day after that. We find it difficult to remain mindful of today because we are concentrating on future days. We are intriguing creatures of God—we live in a past which we can't do anything about, or in a future of which we are not guaranteed.

In all relationships, we will sooner or later encounter a friend who needs to unload his or her burdens. The individual may be suffering from severe symptoms of depression, stress, and/or anxiety. The person needs our undivided attention to hear their burdens and at times possibly to give suggestions on handling the warfare of the depression, stress, and anxiety that is immobilizing one's life.

Mindfulness is living in the moment, ever mindful of whom we are with. When we give our full attention to such a person, then we are giving them one of the highest known compliments... ever. Whatever the friend is saying or doing, we need to put our personal agenda on hold. The friend becomes our center of attention as we are drawn into his or her world. Our senses connect to the person in a wonderful, loving way. The five senses can connect us to what our friend is going through--bad or good.

Listening wholeheartedly to our friend means our not getting lost in our own situation, and attentive listening does require effort because our mind may be running in all kinds of directions. However, if it does wander off the situation of our friend, don't panic—the mountains aren't going to shake, the streams aren't going to dry up, and Atlanta traffic at 5:00 PM isn't going to become simpler—life will go on. When you and I have wandering minds during a conversation, we are having a normal occurrence. Simply, reign in your thoughts and get back into the present sphere with your friend.

I love you not only for what you have made of yourself, but for what you are making of me.

----Roy Croft

During one's time with a friend, don't keep looking at your watch as if to say, *"Hurry up. I've got to go."* Our friend may be on a drama train heading for disaster. Mindfulness requires patience. If we are fretting over the time, our friend will definitely pick up on our time-anxiety. We need to treat our friend in a way that we'd like to be treated. Try putting yourself in their shoes.

A very important rule to remember when listening to the emotional outpouring of a friend is <u>not</u> to be condescending. Being non-judgmental is essential if you and I want to keep the friends we have. Full acceptance is the requirement in order to be attentive in what one is communicating to us.

When our whole being is involved in another person's whole being, then we are being truthfully mindful in its truest sense.

CHAPTER 19

God In A Relationship

I would be remiss, if in this book, I left out the relationship one has with God. While God is not our "buddy" or "pal," He does possess all the characteristics of friendship that was discussed within these pages. He understands the value of genuine friendship so much that He mentions it in His Word:

Proverbs 18:24—a friend who sticketh closer than a brother

John 15:13—lay down his life for his friend

Proverbs 27:17---a man sharpeneth the countenance of his friend

God's love for us is absolutely unconditional. He gives us genuine affection. He does not play "games" with us mentally, emotionally, or physically. God is real. He doesn't sneak around and frighten us. His divine love is authentic and pure. With God, what you "see" with your soul is who God is—no tricks or gimmicks—unconditional love into eternity.

God also cares for us on the deepest level. When we are

hurting, God is present to comfort and to guide us through the corridors of the heartaches. Like our earthly, real friends, God is not going to leave us. He knows that we are all going to face deplorable situations which are out of our control. God is with us during the calamitous circumstances.

Furthermore, God knows what our life goals are. He clearly understands the depth of our desires. Like a true friend on earth, He will support us as we strive for such successes. However, if He knows that such purposes in life are going to create harm and havoc, God will erect divine roadblocks. We might become angry at not reaching our goals and blame God. The same happens with our local friends who warn us about the goals and withdraw their support. At that point, we may shut the relationship door on such friends, but in our relationship with God, He isn't going to be shocked or angry with all the doors we shut on Him. His infinite love continues.

Have you ever wondered how a perfect God can continue to love us when at times we don't give Him the time of day? Well, the answer is that our relationship with Him is solely based on who and what He is, not on who and what we are. God's relationship and kindness are perfect towards us. It can't change because God is exactly the same yesterday, today, and even tomorrow. If we are no longer feeling close to God in our relationship and friendship, guess who moved? It definitely was not God!

Jesus Christ, the same yesterday, and today, and forever.

---Hebrews 13:8

No one can snap his or her fingers and call forth God in one's presence physically. However, God does give His promise that He will always be with us. What a marvelous promise! Here are just a few ways we can maintain our relationship with Him:

*Read the Scriptures.

*Spend individual time with Him.

*Spend collective time with Him, such as church services, spiritual retreats, prayer meetings.

*Meditate.

*Talk to Him.

*Listen.

*Praise Him.

Conclusion

What a powerful concept that surrounds the meaning of friendship. It involves commitment, unconditional love, soothing comfort, positive impact, and freedom to be precisely who we are. The dynamics in a friendship are awe-inspiring because we, in turn, become dedicated to offer our relationship to others. Perhaps my favorite adage is the following:

It's the unexpected kindness from the unexpected person at the unexpected moment that makes someone feel special.

---anonymous

It is my goal and purpose in life to do some kindness for individuals that will touch them with the hope that it tells the persons of just how special they are in my life. Furthermore, I like especially doing it at an unexpected moment in time. Their reaction is usually priceless.

Such is the joy of friendship—doing something positive for someone with no expectations of a return gesture.

BIBLIOGRAPHY

Leal, Bento C. *Four Essential Keys to Effective Communication.* www.bentoleal.com. 2017.

Rosenberg, Marshall B. *Nonviolent Communication.* Encinitas, CA: Puddle Dancer Press, 2015.

Scofield, C. I. (ed). *The New Scofield Reference Bible.* Oxford Press, 1967.

Shumway, Kyler. *The Friendship Formula.* Columbia: Kyler Shumway Publishers, 2018.